CW00821367

JANET O

was born in London and studied languages and linguistics at the University of Edinburgh, and the University of London Institute of Education. Her poetry, short fiction, and life writing have appeared in various publications including *Wasafiri*, *Litro*, *Bare Fiction*, *Far Off Places*, and *Poems on the Buses.* She has authored several children's books, among them *Twins*, *Mr. Football*, and *The Sunbird Mystery*. For adults she has published two short-story collections, *A Brief History of Several Boyfriends* and *The Book of Reasonable Women*, and a novel, *A Traveller's Guide to Namisa*. Her poetry collection *After the Fire* was shortlisted for the Cinnamon Pamphlet Award 2022. She is a graduate of the Manchester Writing School at MMU and the founder of the Abu Dhabi Writers' Workshop. She has lived and worked in Italy, Poland, Oman, and the United Arab Emirates. She now lives in Central Portugal.

Read more at: www.janetolearski.com

Also by Janet Olearski

GROWN-UPS

Poems

Janet Olearski

Copyright © Janet Olearski 2024

The right of Janet Olearski to be identified as the Author of the Work has been asserted by her in accordance with the Copyright, Designs and Patents Act 1988.

All rights reserved. No part of this publication may be reproduced, stored in a retrieval system, or transmitted, in any form or by any means, electronic, mechanical, photocopying, recording or otherwise, without the prior written permission of the copyright owner.

ISBN 978-989-53633-6-0 (Paperback)
ISBN 978-989-53633-7-7 (Ebook)

This book is a work of fiction. Names, characters, places and incidents are a product of the author's imagination or are used fictitiously, and any resemblance to actual persons living or dead, events or locales is entirely coincidental.

Book Cover Design: EBookLaunch https://ebooklaunch.com
Photo by: Ann Danilina on Unsplash

Book Design by: Andrea Reider www.reiderbooks.com

For Glenn Hellman, poet and sculptor.
Short poems, long friendship.

Contents

***

Old School

We passed the shuttered shop in Kensington,
where our mothers bought our school uniforms.
She remembered the ugly slip-on shoes.
I recalled, with reluctance, the straw hats.
I had the shoes, but never had the hat.
My parents couldn't ever stretch to one.
We both remembered the cherry blazers.

The past was hateful and, we both agreed,
to be forgotten. Our old convent school,
she observed, was converted into flats
though the entrance hall had been maintained with
the very same oil painting on the wall.
And that she knew, she said, because chancing
that way, she'd once peered through the letter box.

Point Of View

Then there was a war.
It reminded her
of how they talked once
on the radio
about a war in
a strange-sounding place.
She wanted to know
would they hear gunfire
at home in England?
A war was about
loud explosions, the
sounds of guns firing.
That much she knew. So
it seemed obvious
they would hear the blasts,
even see the smoke
if they stood on their
rooftop in London.
They said no. They laughed.
No, she wouldn't see
or hear anything.
And she thought what a

strange thing war must be.
There would be no smoke.
Nothing would be heard.
Only, just maybe,
something might be felt.

Past Passed

Often it is good
to acknowledge the past, but
not to reclaim it.

The Disappeared

They were promising these
young lads from posh families,
but it seems they came to nothing.

No Facebook profiles.
No X-ful tweets.
Insta-less and un-Linked-In.

So glad I never married one.

Noted

And here is a photo of me,
staring enigmatically into
the eyes of
my now dead cat.
I look lovely,
maybe a little bit sad.
You will feel sorry for me,
for sure.

And what do you think
of this photo of me
as a small and quite
delightful child,
sitting on the lap of
my now dead mother?
You will admire me,
for sure.

And here I am yet again,
my image juxtaposed with
my mother's at the age I am now.
She is magnificent and, for this,
I await your judgement of me.
We are so alike.
This you will agree,
for sure.

And now, for
my new profile picture,
which of these
twenty-two fairly stunning
photos of me
do you think is the best?
For sure you will concur
I turned out well.

Overthinking

She reflects. And when
she reflects, she realizes
that she is alone.

And knowing that she
is alone makes her sad so,
alone, she reflects.

Optimist

A moonbeam fell
into her tree,
but when she went
to rescue it
in the morning,
it was gone.

Knives

When she washes knives
in the kitchen sink,
she separates them,
so they will not fight.

The Purpose Of Waves

Strange that no one lies
this close to the water.
The waves build banks.
She hears them,
busy with their work.

She cannot see the water's edge,
but when she is not looking,
a wave jumps the bank
and tries to reach her
and drag her back. For this,

she believes, it is important to know
the purpose of waves

Doctors

The reason
she hates doctors
is because
they disempower
and control
you. And, just like
hairdressers,
mostly always
get it wrong.

Look

how widely I've travelled,
how well I've eaten,
how clever are my life choices,
how much more I have than you,

how you're missing out while I am not,
how much more I enjoy myself than you,
how original I am,
how boldly I speak my mind,

how I have suffered,
how sad I am because loved ones and pets have died,
how much of a hero I am through adversity,
how much I am envied,

how badly I was treated when I deserved more,
how others have validated me,
how wealthy and well-connected are my friends,
how famous I am by association,

how I do not look my age,
how physically perfect I am,
how healthy are my habits compared to yours,
how expertly I can do everything I do,

how kind I am to others, and generous too,
how I love animals and rescue them,
how spiritual I am, and other worldly,
how uniquely cultured I am,

how one of a kind I am,
how illustrious are my family members,
how pure is my heritage,
how occasionally multicultural I am to suit,

how I can't live without your admiration and approval,
how, if you delete me, you won't see any of this.

Tedious

I beg you, be not a bore.
A book-I-read-before-you-read-it bore,
a look-at-my-beautiful-selfie bore,
a place-I-visited-before-you bore,
a what-a-lot-I-know bore,
a famous-person-I-met bore,
a what-a-cute-baby-I-was-before bore,
a person-who-finds-me-a-bore bore.

Some Grown-Up Observations

You don't have to get married
since you are already whole.
When in doubt,
it helps to do the next thing.
You won't live long enough
to read all the books you've bought.
Not everything in print
is of value or to be believed.
Experts are not experts,
just people making it up as they go along.
People should be left to decide for themselves
so they won't blame you.
You are not obliged to have children,
but they can be put to use.
Being selfish
may one day save your life.
Time-wasters are needy people
who should be avoided at all costs.
People don't hate you as much
as you think they do.
Apparently random observations
are usually unrequested pieces of advice.
Many poems are not actually poems,
but they're poems if you think they are.

Career

When she
grows up,
she will be
a poet,
because
poems
don't
have to
rhyme
and they
can be
short,
or even
thin.

Guidelines

Write it down quickly as it comes.
You can add detail later. Six verses
would be good if you can manage them.
Edit your poem to make it better.

Remove the first three verses to find
the place where your poem really begins.
Then remove the final three verses, so
you'll better appreciate where it ends.

And now, you'll have a virtual poem that lies
lightly on the page in a collection alongside
other vanished poems of similar quality.

But, beware the editor who urges the tinting
of the pages each in a separate colour. For then
your poem will take on an entirely different tone.

Lit Crit

You are invited to be present in the moment,
to be part of the co-creation of the world,
to experience a little denouement at the end.

See how it is extremely neat, how it gives
a sense of completeness and yet
it can be quite packed, almost mathematical,

and that is very interesting, an incredibly powerful
deployment of white space or even
space of another colour, for it can be very trixey,

though, you will see that it is beautiful,
that it is fabulous, that it is fantastic
that it is often edgy, that it is like Lego.

And, you will discover that this is absolutely
correct, that it only remains for you to go in and
have a read and feel that power for yourself.

Unbeliever

She says she is stunned
her work has been longlisted,
or she says she can't believe
her piece has been selected.

She considered her writing
to be so awful
no one in a million years
would have chosen it
but, knowing how bad it was,
she submitted it anyway

in the event
someone might be
stupid enough
not to see its flaws.

At The Poetry Café

One cannot live by poetry alone.

It nourishes the soul,
but not the pocket.

It enhances insight,
but does not pay the optician.

It amplifies thought,
but does not finance the hearing aids.

It illuminates the mind,
but does not pay the electricity bill.

It shelters the spirit,
but does not pay the mortgage.

It quenches our thirst for meaning.
but does not pay for an iced caramel macchiato,

which, at the poetry café today,
one will, nevertheless, not forgo.

Minority Report

I am looking to submit my best work
to a prestigious competition that
has no entry fee, that is for writers
who are old, are female or similar,
are the daughters of refugees, who are
off-white, but also pinkish in colour,
and slightly blotchy, are horse riders and
cat owners and, as a result, single,
who have been to a private school because
they passed their 11-plus, whose mothers
were dyslexic and worked as cleaners, and
whose fathers, because they were refugees,
knew no grammar and did manual work as
boiler operators even though they
trained for something else in their countries of
origin, whose aunties, from Kingston, cooked
Fricassee Chicken from a recipe
taught to them by their grandmas, wrapped mangos,
if still unripened, in the Daily Mail,
who own an African Grey parrot, and
who speak Italian, as well as English,
together with a smattering of other
languages, who have never signed any

controversial petitions, who have been
blocked on X by some famous writer
or other that they have never met and
now never want to meet. There is no doubt
in my mind that if I were to find such
a competition, my submission would
stand a far better than average chance of
getting published and of winning a prize.

Offspring

I created you.
I sent you into the world.
So, you're on your own.

You are a grown-up
poem now, created by
a grown-up poet.

I will not read you,
will not pay for your submissions.
I am free of you.

Wander if you must
into my thoughts, but beware
the younger poems.

Good For Nothing

Her work was terrible, but
she was one of her kind.
The only one.

So, they lauded her
in her awful-ness.
They promoted her
in her incompetence-ness.
They awarded her
in her mediocre-ness.

And they were glad, because
she was exclusive
in her all-inclusive-ness.

Blocked

I had imagined it to be easy,
but I created nothing of worth,
so I went in search of inspiration
and found this chunk of wood,
a chip, I suppose,
but not off the old block.
And this I placed on my shoulder
so everyone would understand
the difficulty under which I laboured.

Voyage Of Discovery

Bobbing in the cold and choppy ocean,
she grasped at flotsam and jetsam,
clinging on until they disintegrated,
and sank.

Incapable of staying afloat
and, obviously, all at sea,
she perished there, unrescued,
and waterlogged.

Some of us—the clever ones—had built boats,
And, though our voyage was not storm-free,
we chugged on, purposefully, to terra that was firma,
and dry, albeit occasionally arid.

Acquaintances

Ed took Jo sailing.
Once. She threw up in his boat.
The sandwich did it.

Meg was obsessive.
Would never go to funerals.
Only to her own.

Dad came to visit.
In the back of his car, Shay
spied a baby seat.

Kate's here, but don't tell.
pm her. She'll stay secret,
driving her red car.

Released from his phone's
tyranny, Ben woke to cries
of Indian peacocks.

Jeff was helping Ruth,
just because it so happened
she was in his path.

When Sue's father died,
it was her great tragedy.
Freed, but set adrift.

Scrolling on his phone,
Bob missed the dramatic arrival
of the elephants.

On Zoom and Skype, much
enhanced, Em adored herself.
It's early days yet.

Trish thought at length on
the absurd lives of others.
But, what of her own?

FanPeople

And who are these,
their faces unfamiliar?
Friends of friends? Is that so?

I am touched to find them
dazzled, smitten, fascinated
by the lives of others.

But, how cleverly they entered
my home unseen, except by pets,
to examine, inspect, evaluate,
the possessions of others.

Yet, when challenged,
I see them unapologetic, and even
aggrieved, indignant, muttering,
as I show them the door.

Singing For Androids

Moon River. Sing up, sing up.
This is singing for androids.
Androids have no fun in the normal course of things.
I dictate the words. You take them down.

Sing up, sing up.
Open your dreary android mouths.
Your eyes are dark and empty, but singing will make
    you better.
It'll bring a little colour to your waxen cheeks.

Sing up, sing up.
Can't write the words?
What model are you?
Androids come cheap these days.

They sit in rows, their notebooks in their android
    fingers,
opening their mouths,
letting words slide out
on a cloud of tone-deaf humming.
Androids don't sing well,
but music is said to lift their sagging souls.

Sing up, sing up.
Moon River. One more time.
Sing a song for androids,
sing it loud and bold.
Another song is coming your way.
You'll sing it when you're told.

Cocktail

People swimming in a tall glass,
all at different levels,
some circling at the bottom like tadpoles,
some floating at the top on lilos,
with their head and toes bumping
against the sides of the glass.
They spin when you stir them.
I prefer milk shakes myself.

Enlightening

Cyberly you come when I am not looking,
slipping into my in-box, taking me unawares.
You are winding yourself up, you say,
taking everything too seriously,
blowing things up out of all proportion.
And who, you ask, *is rattling your cage?*

Now you tell me it's your turn
to be in a bad mood.

You write to me of people lately dead,
of funerals, of animals recently deceased,
of alcoholic friends who drink and drive,
of children abused, of terminal diseases,
of people who murder their pets,
of toxic neighbours who issue threats.

You terrorize me with your emailed news
of yet another day in Meansville.

It troubles me to learn that I self-wind,
blow up all proportions,
too seriously take things,
rattle about in a cage,
am turned moodily bad,
that I am a person I did not know at all.

You see me better than I see myself.
I see you only by gaslight.

Cross My Heart

Do I ever cross your mind?
Do you get a picture of me in your thoughts?
Do you Google me to see if I am still alive?
Do you click on images and enlarge my photos?

Do you ever remember how unkind you were?
Do you wish it could have been different?
Do you ever think we could have had a life together?
Do you guess that you too have crossed my mind?

Waterworld

They had a boat, but not ordinary,
pea-green and beautiful in a sea of
crystal waves and silver sequined foam. They
were sailing west across velvet waves and
reflected stars and there was money in
the boat, filling its hull, twinkling in the
stern. They had coins wrapped up in a five-pound
note, and they had honey. They had honey
in a large jar with two spoons, and when he
looked at the stars above, he heard himself
singing. He had shiny brown feathers and
played a small guitar. There was love in his
voice, long lingering thoughts of passion and
joy. She looked up at the sails, amazed and
charmed, with the breeze rippling through her fur, and
he sang, plucking the strings as she listened.

Grounds For Separation

Whilst looking after her boyfriend's flat,
she threw away the artificial flowers,
because she thought them wilted.

Bookmarking

She told him she made bookmarks
and sold them. But,
how could a woman
live by bookmarks alone?

His, to her, was
a contribution of pity,
a donation for which she paid,
giving freely of herself.

He knew from instinct,
from feeling, from
the tiny quivering calibrations
of the body,

the soft momentary
discolorations of the skin,
that she lied.
But, then, so did he.

She lies there now,
a marked woman,
the mark being what is left of her
between the pages of his book.

The Older Man

The older man impresses
with his sophistication.
He is notorious. He dazzles.
He attracts
blushes.

For him it is
an accepted thing,
this business of being
extraordinary, unprecedented,
blessed, the centre of
attraction.

Until expiry.

Me Too

The lion's den you
enter, knowing. Then emerge
torn, and wondering why.

Misleading

He led her up the garden path
and left her there,
without a return ticket.

Words' Worth

Watch my flower lips,
pale with the dust
I can't see you for.

Spell Of The Betrayed

May the faithless lover
enjoy his own adversity,
and mirror back
his treachery.
For my love,
discarded as a whim,
the harm done me
I now return to him.

Dating Tip

Accept presents
from admirers,
then send them home
with a smile
and a nod.

The Vengeance Of The Fishes

She loved fish. He hated fish.
They suffered fish incompatibility,
fish-watching forbidden,
secret dreams taboo
of fish, grilled or fried.
Even his cats were,
of necessity, carnivorous,
not fishivorous.

Ever observant
of a careless fish word
dropped in error, she suffered
an inqui-fish-tion.
She ate only the loaves
and never the fishes.
She became
de-fish-ent and fish-orexic.

When they split up,
no, she was not gutted,
though she should have
posted a late fish
through his letterbox.
But, know that fish
take their own revenge
for rejection,

sending him
as guest of honour
to his admirers
in Japan. So now,

let her away to celebrate,
his sushi nightmare,
returning like a long-lost friend
to her favourite fish restaurant.

Educating Peter

Woman, this man who asked you out,
does he not know who you are?

Does he not appreciate your cleverness,
how your head is full of facts
and your research is published to acclaim?

Does he not understand that business
should not be mixed with romance,
and your emails are work specific?

Does he not see that you are serious
and focused, that you have no time
for dilly-dallying with the likes of him?

Does he not comprehend that he should not
speak to you before being spoken to,
that he should lower his eyes when you approach?

Does he not know his place, the pecking order,
that he should always walk behind you
on your way to the conference room?

God forbid that he should come close,
or touch you, even accidentally,
his hand lightly brushing yours.

Woman, he is oblivious to the rules,
untutored. Would it help, do you think,
if you asked to speak to his mother?

Body Language

When was it she first noticed her body
was changing? Very slight and very slow
were the variations. But this she did
recall, in that enslaving ritual,
the putting on of make-up, one morning
discovering long silky hairs sprouting
from her upper lip, waving, worming their
way from the sides of her mouth, escaping.

Spreading her foundation, coating, creaming,
other hairs she saw emerging like soft
reeds from the pits of her skin, layering
its surface with a mask delicate and
unctuous. For every hair removed, two
would grow in its place. So said her mother,
and soon she would come to believe her. Mothers,
necromancing, they always know.

But there,
you see, weeks passed with nothing happening.
Until. Until in the place of every
missing hair came a sprouting harsh and black,
akin to the beard of a man, or the
pelt even of an animal, creeping
camouflaged, with stealth from the dark forest
behind her house.

And other changes came.
Toenails, previously smooth and straight, grew hard
and ridged, yellowing at the edges, in
the brief period elapsed between one
trip to the pedicurist and another,
elongating, hooking over, tearing,
wearing down her expectations. For how
should a woman address her body's needs?

Soaking, scrubbing feet with diligence, yet
look how the yellowing extends to the
face of each nail, how walking has become
uncomfortable, how horned like hooves they have
curved in on themselves, how each toe has sawed
at the next. A doctor might deduce this,
reduce this to body abuse, a lack
of maintenance

by she who once reveled
in narcissism, and whose pedicure
that was, on Saturday, so perfect in execution,
was eliminated by the Tuesday
after, such was the rate of growth and the
loathsome shape they took, these talons, these claws.
To wake in the night, to the chafing and
ripping of bedsheets,

to the excessive
warmth of blossoming fur, to the rarest
of desires, incomprehensible, in
both spirit and flesh. Who could not ever
acknowledge the change demanded by this
body? Who could define the nature and
intention of the transformation? Was
blame to be attributed?

No beast was
there in her that she could see. For us all,
there never is. But just a precaution,
then, when waking in the morning, to pray
after incitement that all will again
be normal, and feel an urgency to
check in the mirror to see what she has
become,

and to challenge those sharpened eyes,
the rusted malodorous incisors,
the erect and bristling ears, the twitching
nose, even now trembling as, below, the
carpenter, at work on her kitchen shelves,
misses a nail with his hammer, and draws
blood.

BabySong

She listens to how
they sing their babysong,
twanging the strings of her heart
for the love of a child
she never had.

Anniversaire

I'm wishing you a happy birthday but,
to be honest, we weren't supposed to get
old. We were supposed to stay forever
the same age, probably just twenty-two,
or twenty-three. Something went wrong, you see,
in God's heavenly accounting system.

Talk-less

Let us not talk of death.
Oh, but there I go again.

I will not talk of death
to you, since you are
over sixty-five and an orphan,
and your parents had short lives.

I will not talk of death
to you whose best friend
has just died and she,
as we are both aware, was
so much younger than you.

I will not talk of death
by telling you that the only event
of interest for me last week
was an online funeral.

No, I'd better not mention that,
or even any of the rest.

Facing Reality

I look terrible today.
Will my face always be this way?
Is this the start of my decline,
or merely its continuation?
It's simply that - crumpled - my face
got out of the wrong side of the bed.

Let this not be the face of my obituary.
I will not be there to convince you that
I usually looked better than this.
It was just this one occasion.

Yes, it shows signs of irritation.
It has slipped and been let loose.
Give it time and it will realign.
Whatever our differences, we can make-up.

Uzbekistan

Charles visited Uzbekistan
and posted about it on Facebook.
Christine said Uzbekistan was a beautiful country,
having got there before Charles.
Martin said he visited in 1986, so he saw it first.
No, he did not,
because Graham visited in '82,
and it was even more beautiful then.

I have never been to Uzbekistan,
though I have been to Brighton,
and that is beautiful too.

My friend Rosie tripped and broke her leg
while sightseeing in Uzbekistan.
She did not think it beautiful, but it probably was.

Unsociable Media

I am old and out of the race, unless
I choose to re-enter, which is I think
unlikely, so possibly, certainly,
yes, uncharacteristically, I press
unfollow, unfriend, delete. Why follow
when you are not followed? Why be a friend
to those who care not a fig for you, and
why hover, admiring those who of your
existence are unaware, believing
you a deletion? So, delete them now.
They never cared for you. Why should you care
for them? Decide now that it is over,
really over. There are different paths to
take, not necessarily those others
would want. These are your paths, not the paths of
those so desperate not to be forgotten.
It takes courage to step out into the
snow. Should you leave the group? Yes, it's over.

Old Rage

Do not descend into bitterness,
my friend. You had your chance.
It came and went.

You were going to change the world,
like others before you,
yet your work is incomplete

or, even, never begun.
Your talk was all hot air
and still it scalds.

Should we admire you for your anger,
award you a medal
like the ones you scorn?

Should we say you left this earth,
just you, in disappointment,
acknowledging its unworth?

Look how your grey hairs bristle.
See how your curled-at-the-edges ears
burn at the divine right of others.

Such a mercy you were not born royal.
To save face, register your dismay.
We will look the other way.

Have us understand simply that
you did everything you could,
but no one listened.

Oldness

My hearing is blurred.
My sight is muffled.
Growing old is quite absurd.

I Am Lost

I am lost in a shopping mall.
I've food for several weeks,
and a credit card and some Australian wine,
and there is air and light and sound around,
but my heart goes forward gravely.
For, as I wheel my trolley round,
between the shelves and racks,
I know my body will be found
one day among the stacks
of flour and powdered gravy.

So, if you find this tin of beans,
you'll know exactly what it means:
that I am lost in a shopping mall
and I need someone to save me.

Loved One

After I die,
you will hear my voice.
Then you will know,
more than I loved you,
I loved the parrot.

Pet Project

I want you to
bury me
next to my cat.
Our bones will
mingle and fuse,
so that I
will be reborn
as Cat Woman.

Mascara

In her youth, she found
any mascara would do
for a dry-eyed heart.

But, become old, she
bought waterproof mascara,
her heart now porous.

Disappointing Ways To Die

She died while...
rewriting her will.
wheeling a trolley around Lidl.
at the dentist's.
watching news from the Middle East.
on the toilet.
reading the last chapter of a Stephen King novel.
collecting dry cleaning.
watching the last episode of The Sopranos.
searching for her symptoms on Google.
having a dream in which...

Goals

She created
a 10-year plan
for her life.
And then, unplanned,
she died.

Who will now live for her
her unlived life?

After

After,
in their house,
among the things
he intended to throw away,
he found
a pair of her shoes.

He took a canvas
and painted a swath of blue
for the sky and the sea
of her eyes,
a rich black for the earth
of her hair,
a splash of green
for the hope on the horizon
of her soul,
a spray of gold
for the warm treasure
of her heart.

And then, in his picture,
he placed her shoes,
so she would forever
walk with him
through the landscape
of his memory.

Machine

Someone dies,
maybe someone
close to you,
someone you love.
An absence.
The world goes on
without them.

Something For Later

You do not understand your mother's tears
for the sorrows of others.
Why are sobs suppressed? Why the reddened eyes?
You guess the knee is jiggling
to distract the heart from its thoughts,
the embarrassment of emotion.

These losses are not her problem.
The TV news is not her concern.
This is not her family. Those are not her children.
The slaughtered father is not hers.
The graves do not hold the ones she loved.

Our years bring us memory and association.
They bring us images of past love.
You are young still, and history-less.
You cannot understand your mother's tears.
Wait, and in time you will earn your own.

Acknowledgements

'Old School' was longlisted for *The Bridport Prize (2021)*; 'Minority Report' was shortlisted for *The Aurora Prize for Poetry (2021)*; 'Cocktail' was first published in *The Arabia Review (2004)*; 'The Vengeance of the Fishes' was performed at the *Thames Festival Feast on the Bridge (2011)*; 'Body Language' appeared in a prose version in *The Book of Reasonable Women (2022)*; 'I Am Lost' was one of the *Poems on the Buses*, a *Big Wide Words* event *(1998)*.

***

AFTER THE FIRE

Poems

Janet Olearski

In Portugal in October 2017, engulfed by flames, 53,000 hectares of land were incinerated, countless businesses were ruined, 500 houses were destroyed, over 250 people were injured. And 50 people died.

The author's house, along with many others, was massively damaged in the fires. Encompassing a range of emotions, this collection of poems charts her coming to terms with the aftermath of the disaster, in an unfamiliar environment, in a new country and, later on, through Covid lockdowns. Here are her expressions of sorrow, solitude, regret, nostalgia, and acceptance, but also happiness, hope, and humour... after the fire.

ISBN: 978-989-53633-0-8 (Paperback)
ISBN: 978-989-53633-1-5 (Ebook)

Printed in Poland
by Amazon Fulfillment
Poland Sp. z o.o., Wrocław

46876736R00050

Printed in Poland
by Amazon Fulfillment
Poland Sp. z o.o., Wrocław

46876736R00050